TRANSCENDING RACE IN AMERICA
BIOGRAPHIES OF BIRACIAL ACHIEVERS

Halle Berry

Beyoncé

David Blaine

Mariah Carey

Frederick Douglass

W. E. B. Du Bois

Salma Hayek

Derek Jeter

Alicia Keys

Soledad O'Brien

Rosa Parks

Prince

Booker T. Washington

BEYONCÉ

Singer-Songwriter, Actress, and Record Producer

Chuck Bednar

Mason Crest Publishers

Produced by 21st Century Publishing and Communications, Inc.

MASON CREST PUBLISHERS INC.
370 Reed Road
Broomall, Pennsylvania 19008
(866) MCP-BOOK (toll free)
www.masoncrest.com

Printed in the United States of America.

First Printing

9 8 7 6 5 4 3 2 1

Library of Congress Cataloging-in-Publication Data

Bednar, Chuck, 1976–
    Beyoncé / Chuck Bednar.
       p. cm. — (Transcending race in America : biographies of biracial achievers)
    Includes bibliographical references and index.
    ISBN 978-1-4222-1607-1 (hardback : alk. paper) — ISBN 978-1-4222-1621-7 (pbk. : alk. paper)
    1. Beyoncé, 1981–   —Juvenile literature. 2. Singers—United States—Biography—Juvenile literature. I. Title.
ML3930.K66B43 2010
782.42164092—dc22
[B]   2009022040

Table of Contents

AND THE WINNER IS . . .

Yet when the envelope was opened and the winner was announced, it was indeed Beyoncé whose name was called. Clad in a gorgeous black and white dress, she **ascended** to the stage to accept the prestigious award with her typical quiet grace and humility.

When Beyoncé was asked to sing at the NAACP Image Awards in 2009, she was not only being honored for her distinctive and powerful singing style but also for her career achievements. She has been amazingly successful as a singer, business woman, model, and actress.

> " I HAVE BROTHERS, SISTERS, NIECES, NEPHEWS, UNCLES, AND COUSINS, OF EVERY RACE AND EVERY HUE, SCATTERED ACROSS THREE CONTINENTS, AND FOR AS LONG AS I LIVE, I WILL NEVER FORGET THAT IN NO OTHER COUNTRY ON EARTH IS MY STORY EVEN POSSIBLE. "

> " WE MAY HAVE DIFFERENT STORIES, BUT WE HOLD COMMON HOPES. . . . WE MAY NOT LOOK THE SAME AND WE MAY NOT HAVE COME FROM THE SAME PLACE, BUT WE ALL WANT TO MOVE IN THE SAME DIRECTION — TOWARDS A BETTER FUTURE . . . "

— BARACK OBAMA, 44TH PRESIDENT OF THE UNITED STATES OF AMERICA

As Beyoncé accepted her award for Outstanding Female Artist at the 2 NAACP Image Awards, it truly was her night to shine. In addition to th award, her CD had been nominated for Outstanding Album, a single had nominated for Outstanding Song, and she gave an incredible live perfor that wowed the audience.

1

~❀~

HER NIGHT TO SHINE

AS AN INTERNATIONALLY RECOGNIZED recording artist, Beyoncé was no stranger to appearing in front of crowds. However, things were a little different on February 12, 2009. When she took the stage at the Shrine Auditorium in Los Angeles that night—she had just been honored as the Outstanding Female Artist during the 2009 NAACP Image Awards.

It had been an incredible night all-around for the 27-year-old performer. Her most recent CD, *I Am . . . Sasha Fierce*, had been **nominated** for Outstanding Album, and her song "Single Ladies (Put a Ring on It)" was one of five tracks up for the Outstanding Song award. Also, Beyoncé had a pair of music videos nominated for top honors in that category. She had also been a performer at the show, kicking things off in style by delivering an incredible live version of her song "Halo" that wowed all in attendance.

Of course, being named the Outstanding Female Ar the Year was the icing on the cake for Beyoncé. She was five women up for the honor, and the competition was fie win, she needed to overcome former *Dreamgirls* co-star J Hudson, as well as the talented trio of Alicia Keys, Carey, and Rihanna.

> **"I'd like to thank the NAACP Awards for this beautiful honor, and all the other amazing females that were nominated. I have to say that I'm so, so very blessed to have my family. . . . I want to thank you guys for always being honest with me, keeping me humble, and keeping me human . . . keeping my life in perspective."**

The NAACP Image Awards

On February 12, 2009, the National Association for the Advancement of Colored People (NAACP) presented the 40th Image Awards. Each year, the Image Awards honor outstanding achievements in African-American music, film, television, and literature. The 2009 ceremony, which was broadcast live on the Fox television network, also celebrated the 100th anniversary of the NAACP as an organization.

In addition to Beyoncé, many other noteworthy celebrities were honored at the prestigious event. Jennifer Hudson was named Outstanding New Artist and also won Outstanding Album, while Jamie Foxx won for Outstanding Male Artist. *The Secret Life of Bees* was named the year's best motion picture, while Will Smith and Rosario Dawson won Outstanding Actor and Actress honors for their roles in *Seven Pounds*. In television categories, Tyler Perry's *House of Payne* won for best comedy series, while *Grey's Anatomy* received the honor of being named as the top drama.

For Beyoncé, winning Outstanding Female Artist at the Image Awards was not only a chance to thank those closest to her. It also served as recognition for what had already been an incredible career. Prior to receiving or even being nominated for the award, she had enjoyed considerable success in the roles of singer, songwriter, actress, spokesperson, businesswoman, cover model, and **philanthropist**.

HITTING ALL THE RIGHT NOTES

Before setting out on her own, Beyoncé was a member of the group Destiny's Child. Together they recorded four albums that combined sold more than 30 million copies worldwide and attracted a legion of fans. She followed that up with a pair of solo projects that sold over 14 million copies globally.

NIP/TUCK
Designing a Perfect Body

VOGUE

APR

SHAPE
ISSUE

Fashion for
Every Figure

From
Size 0 to
Size 20

WORK IT!
Longer Legs,

Real Women
Have Curves
BEYONCÉ
At Her Best

In addition to her musical and acting triumphs, Beyoncé has graced many magazine covers and endorsed several well-known products. She has been inspired by other successful female singers and in turn is an inspiration to young people with her involvement with worthy charities.

Her most recent album was released in November 2008 and has already been certified double-platinum by the Recording Industry Association of America (RIAA). One of the main reasons for her tremendous success in the music industry, notes Jody Rosen of *Entertainment Weekly*, is her distinctive and powerful voice.

> **"You'd have to search far and wide—perhaps in the halls of the Metropolitan Opera—to find a vocalist who sings with more sheer force. . . . No one—not R. Kelly, not Usher, to say nothing of her rival pop divas—can match Beyoncé's genius for dragging her vocal lines against a hip-hop beat."**

MORE THAN A MUSICIAN

Of course, Beyoncé's success has not been limited to the world of music. As an actress, she had starred in such hit movies as *Austin Powers in Goldmember*, *Dreamgirls*, and *Cadillac Records*. Her on screen performances have netted her nominations from the NAACP Image Awards, the Kids' Choice Awards, the MTV Movie Awards, the Screen Actors Guild Awards, and the Teen Choice Awards. In an interview with ivillage.co.uk, she said that the inspiration for her acting career comes from other female singers who have walked the same path.

> **"I would have to say Barbra Streisand and Diana Ross in *Mahogany* and all the other movies. They were singers and they were successful and did not have to act, financially or for any other reasons, but they did because they wanted to and they loved it and were talented and gifted at it."**

In addition to her acting and singing careers, Beyoncé has appeared on the cover of countless magazines, become a spokeswoman for a number of well-known products, worked closely with several charities, and pursued a variety of other business ventures. She may have been honored as the Outstanding Female Artist at the 2009 NAACP Image Awards, but clearly her achievements beyond the world of music can be labeled outstanding as well.

A
MUSICAL
PRODIGY

BEYONCÉ GISELLE KNOWLES WAS BORN ON September 4, 1981, in Houston, Texas. She was the first child of Mathew and Tina Knowles. Beyoncé's father is African American. He was born in 1952 and raised in Gaston, Alabama. On the other hand, Tina was born in 1954 in Galveston, Texas. Her family was of Creole descent.

Mathew Knowles attended Fisk University in Nashville, Tennessee. After graduating in 1974, he went on to sell medical equipment such as MRI machines and CT scanners for the Xerox Corporation. Tina grew up in a poor family where her mother had to design robes and altar cloths for a nearby church to earn tuition so that Tina and her siblings could attend a private school. Tina later ran her own salon, called Headliners. The skills Beyoncé's parents learned throughout their lives allowed them to play a major role in their daughter's success later on.

NIP/TUCK
Designing a Perfect Body

V♀GUE

APR

SHAPE
ISSUE
Fashion for
Every Figure
From
Size 0 to
Size 20

WORK IT!
Longer Legs,

Real Women
Have Curves
BEYONCÉ
At Her Best

In addition to her musical and acting triumphs, Beyoncé has graced many magazine covers and endorsed several well-known products. She has been inspired by other successful female singers and in turn is an inspiration to young people with her involvement with worthy charities.

Her most recent album was released in November 2008 and has already been certified double-platinum by the Recording Industry Association of America (RIAA). One of the main reasons

> "I'd like to thank the NAACP Awards for this beautiful honor, and all the other amazing females that were nominated. I have to say that I'm so, so very blessed to have my family. . . . I want to thank you guys for always being honest with me, keeping me humble, and keeping me human . . . keeping my life in perspective."

The NAACP Image Awards

On February 12, 2009, the National Association for the Advancement of Colored People (NAACP) presented the 40th Image Awards. Each year, the Image Awards honor outstanding achievements in African-American music, film, television, and literature. The 2009 ceremony, which was broadcast live on the Fox television network, also celebrated the 100th anniversary of the NAACP as an organization.

In addition to Beyoncé, many other noteworthy celebrities were honored at the prestigious event. Jennifer Hudson was named Outstanding New Artist and also won Outstanding Album, while Jamie Foxx won for Outstanding Male Artist. *The Secret Life of Bees* was named the year's best motion picture, while Will Smith and Rosario Dawson won Outstanding Actor and Actress honors for their roles in *Seven Pounds*. In television categories, Tyler Perry's *House of Payne* won for best comedy series, while *Grey's Anatomy* received the honor of being named as the top drama.

For Beyoncé, winning Outstanding Female Artist at the Image Awards was not only a chance to thank those closest to her. It also served as recognition for what had already been an incredible career. Prior to receiving or even being nominated for the award, she had enjoyed considerable success in the roles of singer, songwriter, actress, spokesperson, businesswoman, cover model, and **philanthropist**.

HITTING ALL THE RIGHT NOTES

Before setting out on her own, Beyoncé was a member of the group Destiny's Child. Together they recorded four albums that combined sold more than 30 million copies worldwide and attracted a legion of fans. She followed that up with a pair of solo projects that sold over 14 million copies globally.

AND THE WINNER IS . . .

Yet when the envelope was opened and the winner was announced, it was indeed Beyoncé whose name was called. Clad in a gorgeous black and white dress, she **ascended** to the stage to accept the prestigious award with her typical quiet grace and humility.

When Beyoncé was asked to sing at the NAACP Image Awards in 2009, she was not only being honored for her distinctive and powerful singing style but also for her career achievements. She has been amazingly successful as a singer, business woman, model, and actress.

As Beyoncé accepted her award for Outstanding Female Artist at the 2009 NAACP Image Awards, it truly was her night to shine. In addition to that award, her CD had been nominated for Outstanding Album, a single had been nominated for Outstanding Song, and she gave an incredible live performance that wowed the audience.

Of course, being named the Outstanding Female Artist of the Year was the icing on the cake for Beyoncé. She was one of five women up for the honor, and the competition was fierce. To win, she needed to overcome former *Dreamgirls* co-star Jennifer Hudson, as well as the talented trio of Alicia Keys, Mariah Carey, and Rihanna.

Chapter

1

HER NIGHT TO SHINE

AS AN INTERNATIONALLY RECOGNIZED recording artist, Beyoncé was no stranger to appearing in front of crowds. However, things were a little different on February 12, 2009. When she took the stage at the Shrine Auditorium in Los Angeles that night—she had just been honored as the Outstanding Female Artist during the 2009 NAACP Image Awards.

It had been an incredible night all-around for the 27-year-old performer. Her most recent CD, *I Am . . . Sasha Fierce*, had been **nominated** for Outstanding Album, and her song "Single Ladies (Put a Ring on It)" was one of five tracks up for the Outstanding Song award. Also, Beyoncé had a pair of music videos nominated for top honors in that category. She had also been a performer at the show, kicking things off in style by delivering an incredible live version of her song "Halo" that wowed all in attendance.

" I HAVE BROTHERS, SISTERS, NIECES,
NEPHEWS, UNCLES, AND COUSINS,
OF EVERY RACE AND EVERY HUE,
SCATTERED ACROSS THREE CONTINENTS,
AND FOR AS LONG AS I LIVE,
I WILL NEVER FORGET THAT
IN NO OTHER COUNTRY ON EARTH
IS MY STORY EVEN POSSIBLE. "

" WE MAY HAVE DIFFERENT STORIES,
BUT WE HOLD COMMON HOPES. . . .
WE MAY NOT LOOK THE SAME
AND WE MAY NOT HAVE
COME FROM THE SAME PLACE,
BUT WE ALL WANT TO MOVE
IN THE SAME DIRECTION —
TOWARDS A BETTER FUTURE . . . "

— BARACK OBAMA, 44TH PRESIDENT
OF THE UNITED STATES OF AMERICA

for her tremendous success in the music industry, notes Jody Rosen of *Entertainment Weekly*, is her distinctive and powerful voice.

"You'd have to search far and wide—perhaps in the halls of the Metropolitan Opera—to find a vocalist who sings with more sheer force. . . . No one—not R. Kelly, not Usher, to say nothing of her rival pop divas—can match Beyoncé's genius for dragging her vocal lines against a hip-hop beat."

MORE THAN A MUSICIAN

Of course, Beyoncé's success has not been limited to the world of music. As an actress, she had starred in such hit movies as *Austin Powers in Goldmember, Dreamgirls,* and *Cadillac Records.* Her on-screen performances have netted her nominations from the NAACP Image Awards, the Kids' Choice Awards, the MTV Movie Awards, the Screen Actors Guild Awards, and the Teen Choice Awards. In an interview with ivillage.co.uk, she said that the inspiration for her acting career comes from other female singers who have walked the same path.

"I would have to say Barbra Streisand and Diana Ross in *Mahogany* and all the other movies. They were singers and they were successful and did not have to act, financially or for any other reasons, but they did because they wanted to and they loved it and were talented and gifted at it."

In addition to her acting and singing careers, Beyoncé has appeared on the cover of countless magazines, become a spokeswoman for a number of well-known products, worked closely with several charities, and pursued a variety of other business ventures. She may have been honored as the Outstanding Female Artist at the 2009 NAACP Image Awards, but clearly her achievements beyond the world of music can be labeled outstanding as well.

Chapter
2

❧ ✾ ❧

A
MUSICAL
PRODIGY

BEYONCÉ GISELLE KNOWLES WAS BORN ON September 4, 1981, in Houston, Texas. She was the first child of Mathew and Tina Knowles. Beyoncé's father is African American. He was born in 1952 and raised in Gaston, Alabama. On the other hand, Tina was born in 1954 in Galveston, Texas. Her family was of Creole descent.

Mathew Knowles attended Fisk University in Nashville, Tennessee. After graduating in 1974, he went on to sell medical equipment such as MRI machines and CT scanners for the Xerox Corporation. Tina grew up in a poor family where her mother had to design robes and altar cloths for a nearby church to earn tuition so that Tina and her siblings could attend a private school. Tina later ran her own salon, called Headliners. The skills Beyoncé's parents learned throughout their lives allowed them to play a major role in their daughter's success later on.

Beyoncé was called a prodigy because she developed her musical skills so young. Her family, which is of mixed African-American and Creole descent, started to encourage her when they first saw her talent blossoming in the church choir at the age of seven.

Beyoncé and her family have long embraced their racial heritage. Her father grew up in the South during the era of **segregation**, and had to overcome more than his share of race-related struggles. Her maternal grandparents spoke French and lived in New Orleans, Louisiana, before relocating to Texas. Beyoncé's mother, Tina, was born Celestine Ann Beyincé, and in fact Beyoncé's name was a tribute to her mother's maiden name and her Creole ancestry.

DISCOVERING HER GIFT

In some ways, Beyoncé's childhood was fairly normal. She went to St. Mary's Elementary School, and along with her parents and her younger sister Solange, regularly attended St. John's United Methodist Church. Beyoncé sang in the church's choir, and it was during these services that people started to first take notice of her ability and passion for music. For a young child, she worked incredibly hard developing her raw talent and even started performing by the age of seven.

Of course, that didn't mean that growing up was all work and no play for the budding **diva**. She still had some time left over for relaxation and normal childhood activities, as she later noted on the Greater Houston Convention and Visitors Bureau Web site:

> "Growing up in Houston was fun. We always had a huge backyard to play in. My mom allowed my friends to come over all the time; it was like a continuous slumber party at our house. I spent my summers going to AstroWorld, SplashTown. . . . I had a great childhood in Houston!"

Still, it was clear early on that Beyoncé had a musical gift. It didn't take long before she became a soloist in the St. John's

About Louisiana Creole People

Beyoncé's mother Tina and her maternal grandparents (Lumis Albert Beyincé and Agnéz Deréon) were of Louisiana Creole descent. The term Louisiana Creole refers to people who are of mixed French, African-American, and Native-American blood. The term dates back to the 16th century and was originally used to refer to descendents of French, Spanish, or Portuguese origin.

Over four million people of Louisiana Creole ancestry currently live in the United States. Other famous individuals who come from Creole backgrounds include boxer Laila Ali (the daughter of the legendary Muhammad Ali), professional basketball player Grant Hill, former *The Today Show* host Bryant Gumbel, rapper and actor Ice-T, and musicians Fats Domino and Jelly Roll Morton.

choir. She not only attended dance classes but was also trained in classical opera. In 1988, she competed in her first talent show and performed the classic John Lennon hit "Imagine." She won, and was even given her very first standing ovation. Ultimately, Beyoncé wound up winning more than 30 local and regional awards, all but cementing a bright future as a performing artist.

Beyoncé impressed audiences at an early age. She became a soloist in the church choir, took dance lessons, and trained in classical opera. She won her first talent show, where the roaring crowd gave her a standing ovation. It was just the first step toward her future as a superstar.

At the age of eight, Beyoncé became the lead singer for an all-girl group called Girl's Tyme. They were popular in Houston, but when they appeared on *Star Search* in Hollywood, they lost the competition and a possible record deal. Beyoncé never gave up, though, and kept striving toward a music career.

GIRL'S TYME

At the age of eight, Beyoncé attended an audition for a new all-girl group that was being put together and financed by a woman named Andretta Tillman. Once again, Beyoncé's musical talent was instantly recognizable, and she was asked to be the lead singer for the group. Other members of the group included her cousin, Kelly Rowland, as well as Tamar Davis, LaTavia Roberson, LeToya Luckett, and sisters Nikki and Nina Taylor. Collectively, they were known as Girl's Tyme, and it wasn't too long before their singing, rapping, and dancing started drawing national attention.

In 1992, after performing several successful gigs at festivals, events, and locations in and around the Houston area, they were noticed by rhythm and blues producer Arne Frager. Frager flew them out to California and arranged for them to debut on the hit TV show *Star Search*. The plan was to showcase the girls' talent on national television, then use their winning performance to secure a big-time recording deal. Unfortunately, things didn't exactly work out as planned, as Beyoncé would later recall in an interview with Billy Johnson Jr. of Yahoo! Music.

> **❝** *Star Search* **is a memorable moment. . . . We had been rehearsing forever. It seemed like 100 years . . . and we did the wrong song . . . but regardless, we lost. . . . We couldn't even last until we got backstage; the tears were already falling. We were devastated, we thought our lives were over. But then again, that was my first time I lost something that I really wanted to win. ❞**

Girl's Tyme had enjoyed success locally, but on the national stage, the group faced their share of tough times. They lost *Star Search*, and as a result, they lost a possible record deal. Shortly thereafter, they also lost Andretta Tillman, the driving force behind the group. However, as they say, **adversity** builds character, and there was no doubt that the girls of Girl's Tyme would rebound. It was their destiny.

DESTINY COMES CALLING

FROM THE ASHES OF GIRL'S TYME, DESTINY'S Child rose up, with Beyoncé as the cornerstone. Throughout the second half of the 1990s, the group's story was one of hard work, personal sacrifice, conflict, change, recognition, awards, and unbelievable success. It all started with an incredible gamble on the part of Beyoncé's father, Mathew Knowles.

Mathew was consistently one of the top salesmen at Xerox, and earned more than $100,000 per year selling medical equipment. Yet, in the aftermath of *Star Search*, he saw the talented performers of Girl's Tyme **dejected** and directionless. He felt as though he had to act, so he left his job and took over as the group's manager. With him at the helm, the original lineup was reduced to four— Beyoncé, Kelly Rowland, LaTavia Roberson, and LeToya Luckett. After several name changes, the group decided on a **moniker** inspired by the biblical book of Isaiah. Thus, Destiny's Child was born.

Four members of Girl's Tyme went on to form Destiny's Child. They worked hard and inked a record deal, which later fizzled. Their intense effort finally paid off when their first album debuted in 1998. At last they had a chance to show the world they could be stars.

STRESS AND SUCCESS

While Mathew put his sales skills to work trying to secure a record deal for Destiny's Child, Beyoncé's mother also began working closely with the band. Leaving the management of her salon in the hands of a family friend, Tina began designing outfits for the singers to use during shows and auditions. The quartet apparently had found success, signing with Elektra Records in 1995. However, that turned out to be an illusion, as Destiny's Child (then known as The Dolls) was dropped nine months later. As she told the Entertainment Weekly Web site, Beyoncé was devastated.

"We felt like our life was over. We thought we would never get signed again. "

The first release from Destiny's Child was not as successful as Beyoncé had hoped. While one single on the album was a hit, others did not create the same excitement. However, the girls were only 15, and their developing talent would soon blossom.

The tough times also started to take their toll on her parents' marriage, including numerous disagreements and eventually leading Mathew and Tina to briefly separate during this time. The couple eventually worked out their problems, though, and Destiny's Child forged ahead. The group kept trying, auditioning, and hoping for their big break. Finally, their hard work paid off when, in 1996, Columbia Records signed the group. In 1997, they recorded their first song for their new label. The tune, "Killing Time," was featured in the film *Men in Black*. At long last, all their effort had paid off. Destiny's Child had their chance to prove they could be stars.

DESTINY'S CALL

On February 17, 1998, the girls released their first album for Columbia, the self-titled *Destiny's Child*. Some of the top talent in the music industry worked with them on the album, including Wyclef Jean, Master P, and producers Rob Fusari and Jermaine Dupri. *Destiny's Child* was a mild hit, selling 500,000 copies **domestically** and making it to number 67 on the *Billboard* charts. However, in an interview with writer Paul Flynn of the *Guardian*, Beyoncé confessed that she was somewhat disappointed with the quartet's initial release.

> **❝The first record was successful but not hugely successful. It was a neo-soul record and we were 15 years old. It was way too mature for us.❞**

The biggest hit from the album was a dance remix of the song "No, No, No," entitled "No, No, No Part 2." The song, which also featured Wyclef Jean, peaked at number three on the *Billboard* Hot 100 Chart and earned the group two Soul Train Lady of Soul Awards, including one for Best R&B/Soul Single by a Group, Band, or Duo. "No, No, No" sold more than one million copies, and was later certified platinum by the RIAA. Other singles followed, including "With Me" and "Get on the Bus," but they failed to generate the same level of buzz.

DEVELOPING A STAGE PRESENCE

Despite the recent release of their debut album, Destiny's Child remained hard at work in 1998. They performed as the opening act for Boyz II Men during select concert dates, and did a number of other promotional shows and events as well, including several relatively small-time gigs for radio stations and record stores. However, as one Columbia executive later told *Billboard*, it really didn't matter whether the performance was in front of a large crowd or a small one, because Destiny's Child was always at the top of their game.

> **"They were in a parking lot in front of a department store on a one-foot riser with a stage. Yet those girls came prepared like they were playing Madison Square Garden. They were doing their own hair and makeup, complete with costume changes. . . . There were no lights and cameras. Just them and a crowd of people. And they killed it."**

That kind of extraordinary stage presence didn't just happen. It was something the members of Destiny's Child had worked extremely hard to perfect. As Beyoncé later told Christopher John Farley of *Time* magazine, they drew their deepest inspiration from one of the greatest and most popular female groups of all time, The Supremes.

Who Were The Supremes?

The Supremes were an all-female singing group that featured Diana Ross and Mary Wilson, among other alternating members. The group, which was signed to the Motown record label in 1961, had 12 different songs reach number 1 on the *Billboard* charts, more than any other Motown artist.

Among their most memorable hits were the songs "Stop! In The Name of Love," "Back in My Arms Again," "Come See About Me," and "Baby Love." In 1988, The Supremes were inducted into the Rock and Roll Hall of Fame, and in 2004 they were featured in *Rolling Stone* magazine's "100 Greatest Artists of All Time."

Although not yet recording stars, Destiny's Child continued to impress critics and audiences with their dedication and amazing stage presence in live performances. They took their inspiration from the glamour and intensity of the hugely successful 1960s group, The Supremes.

"I love and respect The Supremes because they were glamorous, and whenever they walked into a room they lit up the room. That's what Destiny's Child tries to do . . . . A lot of people don't have any concept of how many sacrifices we have to make. You have to accept it, because if you don't, you won't last."

THE WRITING'S ON THE WALL

Later in the year, the girls were rushed back into the studio to record a follow-up album. However, by this time, the whirlwind schedule had started to expose some tensions within the group. What had seemingly been one big happy family was slowly starting to dissolve, but Beyoncé, Kelly, LaTavia, and LeToya were able to put personal differences aside long enough to finish work on their second album.

That CD, *The Writing's on the Wall*, was released on July 27, 1999. It debuted at number 6 on the *Billboard* Hot 100 charts, sold more than 130,000 copies in the first week, and went platinum before the end of the year. Two singles from the record, "Bills, Bills, Bills" and "Say My Name," went on to reach the top of the charts. The album became the group's first real hit, and went on to sell more than nine million copies worldwide.

However, not even the album's remarkable success could save Destiny's Child. In December 1999, right before they were to start filming a video for "Say My Name," LaTavia and LeToya sent letters accusing Mathew Knowles of improper conduct and tried to fire him as their manager. Mathew, in turn, replaced them with Michelle Williams and Farrah Franklin, and the video was shot as if nothing happened. Shortly thereafter, Franklin was fired, reportedly because she failed to show up for rehearsals, and LaTavia and LeToya sued over being let go from the band.

CHANGING DESTINY

In the midst of all the chaos, the remaining members of Destiny's Child—Beyoncé, Kelly Rowland, and Michelle Williams—tried to carry on to the best of their abilities. However, it was not easy. Things were especially rough for Beyoncé, who had to deal not only with the departure of two longtime friends and the various accusations against her father, but also charges that Mathew Knowles was trying to make her the focal point of Destiny's Child. As she later told the British Web site Times Online, she dealt with depression during this era.

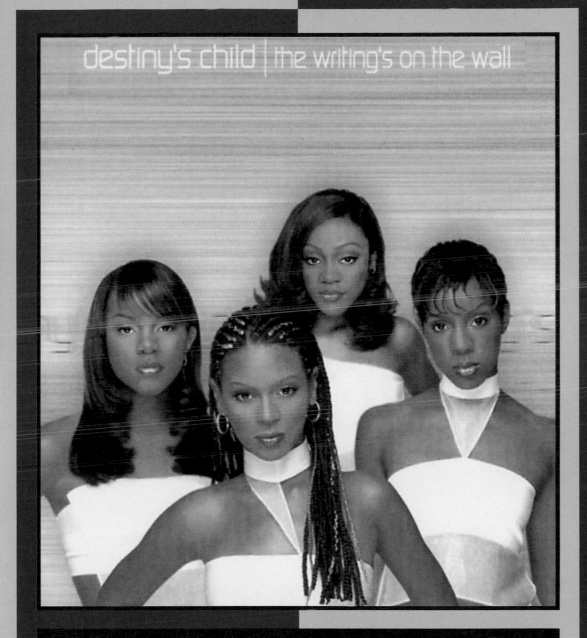

destiny's child | the writing's on the wall

Destiny's Child had their first hit with their second album, *The Writing's on the Wall*, which jumped to number 6 on the charts its first week and went platinum later in 1999. Two singles, "Bills, Bills, Bills" and "Say My Name," also went on to be chart-toppers.

Beyoncé's father, Mathew Knowles, was instrumental in the early success of Destiny's Child, but he also was involved in controversy that threatened the group's future. Beyoncé was discouraged by these challenges, but finally the group, now a threesome, was able to move on and focus on their music.

> **"It was tough. Before that, the media didn't pay attention to me personally: it was just our music. After that, I felt attacked. . . . I went through depression. I was sad. I didn't eat. I stayed in my room. I was in a really bad place in life, going through that lonely period. . . . That's when I decided I only have two choices: I can be depressed and give up, or I can be positive and go on."**

Dealing with Depression

The term depression is often used to describe feeling down in the dumps, but it can actually be a serious medical condition. According to the Mayo Clinic Web site, "It affects how you think and behave and can cause a variety of emotional and physical problems. You may not be able to go about your usual daily activities, and depression may make you feel as if life just isn't worth living anymore."

More than 14 million people in the United States suffer from this type of depression. The good news is that in most cases, it can be easily treated through psychological counseling or the use of medication. If you believe you are currently suffering from depression, or you know someone who is, talk to a medical professional or call the Depression and Bipolar Support Alliance at 1-800-826-3632.

Beyoncé went on, and so did Destiny's Child, although as a trio and not a quartet. The group went on tour, opening for both Britney Spears and Christina Aguilera in support of *The Writing's on the Wall*. Eventually, the lawsuits were settled and the drama subsided, allowing Beyoncé, Kelly, and their new associate Michelle to focus once again on what was really important: the music.

SURVIVOR

THE YEAR 2000 BROUGHT A BREAKOUT FOR Beyoncé in many ways. Destiny's Child won six Billboard Music Awards, including Top Pop Artist, and their video for "Say My Name" was named the Best R&B Video at the MTV Music Awards. Later on, she joined Kelly and Michelle as the trio recorded their first song together, "Independent Women Part 1."

The song appeared on the soundtrack for the movie *Charlie's Angels* and spent 11 consecutive weeks atop the *Billboard* Hot 100 chart. The group was enjoying tremendous success, due largely to Beyoncé's talent and dedication. Executives at Columbia Records noticed, and in October 2000, they rewarded her with a three-album solo deal. First, though, she needed to finish up some business as a member of Destiny's Child: a third album.

In 2000, the new Destiny's Child lineup—Beyoncé, Kelly Rowland, and Michelle Williams—enjoyed huge success as their hit single, "Independent Women Part 1," topped the charts for almost three months. The girls' determination and hard work was clearly paying off for the group.

INSPIRED BY THE PAST

When Beyoncé, Kelly, and Michelle returned to the studio in late 2000 to record *Survivor*, they brought with them their feelings about everything that had happened since the release of their last album. That pent-up emotion wound up being a positive thing, Kelly later told MTV.com, as they managed to tap into it creatively.

"I know everybody can relate to this album—it's very diverse and inspiring. The year 2000 was very challenging, and I know that gave Beyoncé a lot of inspiration to write songs for the album. We cannot wait for everybody to hear it. It's so empowering."

Survivor debuted at number one on the *Billboard* charts, and within three months it reached triple-platinum status. In 2001, the group won their first Grammy Awards, including Best R&B

Destiny's Child had put their difficulties behind them, as they made clear in the title of their next album, *Survivor*. In 2001, *Survivor* went triple platinum and brought the group worldwide recognition and two Grammy Awards. Here the group appears on the German TV show *Wetten Dass* in 2001.

Song for "Say My Name." Beyoncé also became just the second woman ever to win the American Society of Composers, Authors, and Publishers (ASCAP) Songwriter of the Year Award. In October, Destiny's Child released a Christmas-themed album *8 Days of Christmas*, then announced they would be going on **hiatus** to work on solo projects.

ON HER OWN

Ironically, Beyoncé's first major project following the temporary split of Destiny's Child was not a solo album. Rather, it was the role of Foxxy Cleopatra in the Mike Myers film *Austin Powers in Goldmember*. Although she had previously acted in the 2001 made-for-TV musical *Carmen: A Hip Hopera*, this was Beyoncé's first role in a major motion picture. As she later admitted to writer Paul Fischer, she was nervous about the gig.

> **"**I was scared because some singers who become actors get a lot of criticism. I didn't want to be one of those singers who said: Okay, we've sold records, so now I'm going to act. They approached me and I got the part, so it was great. I just wanted to make sure I delivered the right performance.**"**

Her acting performance earned her two Teen Choice Award nominations, one as best crossover star and the other for top female breakout performance. It also helped *Goldmember* debut atop the box office, bringing in more than $70 million during its opening weekend. Music was still very much a part of Beyoncé's life as well, as she contributed the songs "Work it Out" and "Hey Goldmember" to the movie's soundtrack.

Hot on the heels of her film debut, Beyoncé signed an endorsement deal with Pepsi. Her star was definitely on the rise, and her previous efforts as a member of Destiny's Child were still being recognized as well. The group earned another Grammy in 2002, as well as several other awards. Around this time, people also began to **speculate** on her private life. Rumors linked her romantically to hip-hop artist Jay-Z, but the intensely private Beyoncé refused to comment.

Mike Myers and the *Austin Powers* Movies

Born on May 25, 1963, Mike Myers is a Canadian comedian, actor, writer, and producer who gained fame on the NBC sketch comedy program *Saturday Night Live*. In 1989, he won an Emmy for his writing with *SNL*, and in 1992 he made his film debut in *Wayne's World*, a movie based on a popular and whacky character from the show.

Myers debuted the Austin Powers character in 1997's *Austin Powers: International Man of Mystery*, which was an over-the-top spoof of James Bond–style spy movies. Two sequels followed: 1999's *Austin Powers: The Spy Who Shagged Me* and 2002's *Austin Powers in Goldmember*, each of which earned Myers American Comedy Awards for Best Film Performance (Male) and Best Writing.

"CRAZY IN LOVE"

Those rumors persisted as Beyoncé worked on her second movie, a comedy called *The Fighting Temptations* that earned her BET Comedy Award and Image Award nominations for both her acting and her work on the soundtrack. Rumors continued as she expanded her endorsement **portfolio** by signing with L'Oreal. They went on as she teamed with singer Luther Vandross for a Grammy-winning cover of the duet "The Closer I Get to You," and they were fueled when she and Jay-Z **collaborated** on his hit single "'03 Bonny and Clyde."

In truth, the two had been dating since meeting at an awards show the previous year. Despite the fact that she was 12 years younger, the two instantly connected. One friend later told *People* magazine that they were "soul mates." However, they both worked hard to keep their courtship out of the press, preferring to live out their romance in privacy rather than in tabloid headlines. As Beyoncé later told *Essence* magazine,

> **"What Jay and I have is real. It's not about interviews or getting the right photo op. It's real."**

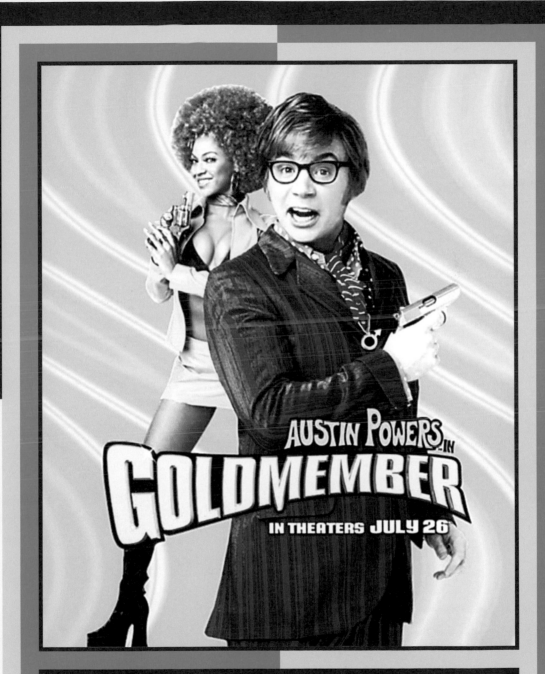

Beyoncé's solo career began with her first acting gig in the film *Austin Powers in Goldmember*. She won two Teen Choice Award nominations for her work and penned two songs for the movie's soundtrack. If that weren't enough to keep her busy, she signed on as the new spokesperson for Pepsi.

Beyoncé's first solo album featured Jay-Z on the single "Crazy in Love." The album sold more than 5 million copies, and Beyoncé and Jay-Z gave a hot performance of the song at the 2003 MTV Video Music Awards. The long-time couple married in 2008.

In June 2003, Beyoncé released her first solo album, ironically entitled *Dangerously in Love*. The album featured a Jay-Z rap on the track "Crazy in Love." The two even performed the track together at the MTV Music Awards that year. *Dangerously in Love* went on to sell more than 5 million copies, spawned a pair of number 1 hits and was later named one of the 100 best albums of the past 25 years by *Entertainment Weekly*.

Jay-Z

Shawn Corey Carter (better known to the world as rap artist and hip-hop mogul Jay-Z) was born on December 4, 1969. He grew up in Brooklyn, New York, and burst onto the music scene with his debut album, *Reasonable Doubt*, in 1996. The CD peaked at number 23 on the *Billboard* charts and was later named one of the 500 greatest records of all time by *Rolling Stone* magazine.

Other Jay-Z albums include *In My Lifetime, Vol. 1*; *Vol. 2 . . . Hard Knock Life*; *Vol. 3 . . . Life and Times of S. Carter*; *The Dynasty: Roc La Familia*; *The Blueprint*; *The Blueprint2: The Gift & the Curse*; *The Black Album*; *Kingdom Come*; and *American Gangster*. He is an eight-time Grammy winner and has sold more than 25 million records over his career.

IN THE SPOTLIGHT

With the remarkable success of *Dangerously in Love*, Beyoncé had surely established herself as a solo artist, and was now in the national spotlight more than ever. In February 2004, she performed the national anthem before the kickoff of Super Bowl XXXVIII at Houston's Reliant Stadium. Beyoncé, who as a child had been inspired by Whitney Houston's moving performance at Super Bowl XXV, told Hannah Storm of CBS that it was an emotional experience,

> **"I was so nervous before I sang the song. My heart, I could see it beating out of my chest, because this has been a dream. And I have been telling my mother since I was, I don't know 8, 9, 'I'm going to do that.' . . . I could hardly fight back the tears."**

For many people, such a performance might be the highlight of an entire year or even a lifetime, but not for Beyoncé, and certainly not in 2004. Later on in the year, Beyoncé won five Grammy Awards, including Best R&B Song ("Crazy in Love"); Best Female R&B Vocal Performance ("Dangerously in Love 2"); and Best Contemporary R&B Album for *Dangerously in Love*. In winning five Grammy Awards in the same year, she tied the record for the most ever awards for a female artist and had clearly established herself as one of the premiere performing artists in the music industry.

DESTINY FULFILLED

Of course, Beyoncé wasn't the only one who had found solo success. The other members of Destiny's Child had as well. Kelly's first album produced a number one hit, "Dilemma," while Michelle's *Heart to Yours* was the best selling gospel album of 2002. With their solo careers off to fantastic starts, in early 2004 the young women decided to reunite for one final album together—a prospect that Beyoncé told Storm she was extremely excited about.

> **"We've all grown so much. We were 19 and now we're 22, 23. We're adults. So a lot of our opinions are different. So it's going to be interesting to see what's going to happen. But I'm so looking forward to it and so are the other ladies."**

Despite rumors that Beyoncé's younger sister would be joining the group, the Destiny's Child lineup remained unchanged as the girls returned to the studio that May to record *Destiny Fulfilled*. The girls wrote nearly all the songs on the album, inspired by conversations that were recorded as they caught up with one another. Beyoncé, Kelly, and Michelle worked tirelessly over a three-week period, crafting songs that were meaningful to each of them and showcased their unique talents. Beyoncé later told MTV.com,

Her 2004 album, *Dangerously in Love*, was a blockbuster hit for Beyoncé and was named one of the 100 best albums of the past 25 years. Golden, glamorous Beyoncé took home five Grammys, tying the record set by Alicia Keys, Norah Jones, and Lauryn Hill for most Grammys won by a female artist.

❝It was important for me, the vocal producer of the record, for people to hear Michelle, to hear how soulful and raspy her voice is. To hear how colorful and clear Kelly's voice is and to hear all of us and how different we are. . . . We wanted to make sure that the songs would be something that we were proud of 10 years from now, 20 years from now.❞

DESTINY'S CHILD SAYS GOODBYE

Destiny Fulfilled was released on November 15, 2004, and sold nearly 500,000 copies during its first official week of availability. It went on to sell more than three million copies in the United States by January 2005. Several tracks on the album enjoyed success, including the Grammy Award–nominated "Lose My Breath" and two hits that achieved RIAA platinum status, "Cater 2 U" and "Soldier." However, some critics, including Tom Sinclair of *Entertainment Weekly*, questioned the move.

❝Over the past several years, we've watched Beyoncé Knowles morph from just another comely singer in a cookie-cutter R&B girl group into, well . . . the only artist around who might pick up Madonna's mantle and lead the way into a bold new future for women in pop. . . . Beyoncé's continued allegiance to Destiny's Child, however, may slow down her progress.❞

Critical opinion aside, Beyoncé was a performer who never forgot where she came from and remained true to her friends. Together she, Kelly, and Michelle followed up their final album by performing together live on the National Football League Opening Kickoff television special, doing promotional work for McDonald's, and then setting off on a world tour. The "Destiny Fulfilled . . . And Lovin' It" tour featured material off the new album, past Destiny's Child hits, and songs from each member's solo albums.

It would be the swan song for the group. Before beginning the U.S. leg of the tour, the members of Destiny's Child officially announced they were breaking up. In a press statement, they stated that they wanted to end things on a high note and with their close, sisterly bond still intact. Over the course of a decade, Destiny's Child sold more than 40 million records and emerged as one of the most popular female groups of all time. But it was simply time to move on.

Destiny's Child proudly brought out their final album and went on a farewell tour in 2005. At the same time, the young divas realized it was time to break up and move on to solo success. Destiny's Child made music history and is still the world's best-selling female group of all time.

One of Beyoncé's new solo ventures was a fashion line, the House of Deréon, which she created with her mother Tina (right). She also showed her business savvy making commercial endorsements, working on a perfume line, and helping set up a charitable foundation to help victims of Hurricane Katrina.

Kelly and Michelle: Where Are They Now?

Like Beyoncé, the other former members of Destiny's Child found musical success in the days and weeks following the band's breakup. Kelly's second solo album, *Ms. Kelly*, was released in June 2007 and was her first CD to crack the *Billboard* top 10. She has also pursued an acting career, including a role in 2004's *The Seat Filler*.

Michelle has also pursued an acting career, including a successful run in the stage production of *The Color Purple*. Michelle is active with a number of charities in the Chicago area and is a co-owner of the Chicago Sky women's basketball team. Her third solo album, *Unexpected*, was released in October 2008.

MOVING ON

In 2005, following the Destiny's Child farewell tour, anticipation for Beyoncé's second album was extremely high. However, the follow-up to *Dangerously in Love* was put on hold as she pursued other projects, including her acting career. Beyoncé landed roles in a pair of upcoming movies during this time, *The Pink Panther* and *Dreamgirls*.

Other ventures occupied her time as well. Beyoncé and her mother Tina teamed up to launch a fashion line, the House of Deréon (named in honor of her maternal grandmother). She continued her endorsement work and started creating perfumes for Tommy Hilfiger. Inspired by the devastation of Hurricane Katrina, she helped set up the Survivor Foundation, which at the time helped Houston area families displaced by the storm but later expanded and became an all-purpose charity.

Her personal life was also going well, as marriage talk swirled about her and Jay-Z. Given their private nature, neither party would address the rumors. Having found success in music, film, business, and romance, it was clear that the now 24-year-old Beyoncé had already enjoyed an amazing life and career. However, the best was yet to come.

INDEPENDENT WOMAN

ALTHOUGH IT HAD BEEN SEVERAL YEARS since the release of the Destiny's Child hit song "Independent Woman, Part I," 2006 saw Beyoncé **epitomizing** that song through her life and career. In January, she and fellow stars Jamie Foxx, Jennifer Hudson, and Eddie Murphy began work filming *Dreamgirls*, and in February, *The Pink Panther* hit theaters across the country.

Despite not being a favorite among critics, *The Pink Panther* opened atop the box office and stayed there for two weeks, grossing more than $60 million during that period. In the film, Beyoncé played the character of Xania, the girlfriend of a murdered soccer player and a suspect in the crime, as well as one of the targets of Inspector Clouseau's (Steve Martin) affections. She also wrote and performed the songs "Check on It" and "A Woman Like Me."

©2005 CTMG

Beyoncé continued to set an example as a bright, independent woman in 2006. She flexed her acting muscles with a comedy role in *The Pink Panther*, with Steve Martin. But her main focus that year was a dream project, the film *Dreamgirls*.

However, while the public enjoyed the movie and her fans were eagerly anticipating a second solo album, Beyoncé's focus for much of early 2006 was squarely on *Dreamgirls*. In the film, which was loosely based on the story of The Supremes, Beyoncé played Deena Jones, a character very similar to real-life Motown legend Diana Ross. From the first, Beyoncé knew that this film would be something special and put her recording career on hold to focus solely on the project at hand. As she told Billboard.com:

In *Dreamgirls*, Beyoncé (center) nailed the part of Deena Jones, in an amazing cast that included Eddie Murphy, Jamie Foxx, and *American Idol* newcomer Jennifer Hudson. Playing Deena set off many emotions, which transformed Beyoncé's songwriting for her next album and gave the recording remarkable depth and style.

"I'm not going to write for the album until I finish doing the movie. I've never been so excited about a movie in my life. I want to give 100 percent to this film, because I know I was born for this role."

Jennifer Hudson and *Dreamgirls*

Based on a 1981 Broadway musical, the 2006 film *Dreamgirls* was co-written and directed by Bill Condon and co-produced by Paramount Pictures and Dream-Works Pictures. It tells the story of the Dreams, a Supremes like female musical group (played by Beyoncé, Jennifer Hudson, and Anika Noni Rose), as they experience relationships, success, and betrayal in their attempt to rise to the top. It was nominated for multiple Academy Awards, winning two, including Best Supporting Actress honors for Jennifer.

Born on September 12, 1981, Jennifer, who played Effie White in the movie, first attracted national attention when she competed on the third season of the popular *American Idol* television program. Following her award-winning performance in *Dreamgirls*, she went on to work in the films *Sex and the City* and *The Secret Life of Bees*. In November, 2006, she signed a recording deal with Arista Records, and her debut album *Jennifer Hudson* was nominated for three Grammy Awards, including Best R&B Album.

SUCCESS ON TWO FRONTS

The decision to focus on *Dreamgirls* first, and then the follow-up album, wound up being a smart move on two fronts. On the one hand, it allowed Beyoncé to devote all her time and effort to the role of Deena Jones. On the other, when filming on the movie wrapped in May and it came time to finally return to recording, she was more than ready, as she told MTV.com:

"I was Deena for six months and I refused to go into the studio 'cause I didn't want to get myself confused with this character. . . . [When filming ended] I had so many things bottled up, so many emotions, so many ideas, that while I was supposed to be on vacation I snuck into the studio and recorded this album in two weeks. . . . I had a lot to say."

That second album, entitled *B'Day*, was released in September 2006, in time for Beyoncé to celebrate her 25th birthday. The album included a mix of musical styles, including blues and funk, and once again featured a cameo from boyfriend Jay-Z on the song "Déjà Vu." *B'Day* was an immediate hit as it debuted atop the *Billboard* Hot 200 Chart and sold more than 540,000 copies in its first week. It also produced her biggest hit, "Irreplaceable," which spent 10 consecutive weeks at number one.

Likewise, *Dreamgirls* was an immediate success as well, bringing in more than $14 million during its December 2006 opening weekend and going on to gross more than $150 million worldwide. The film received eight Oscar nominations in 2007, with Jennifer Hudson winning the Academy Award for Best Supporting Actress. Beyoncé herself received a Golden Globe nomination for her role, and her performance of "Listen" won the Broadcast Film Critics Association Award for Best Song.

AWARDS, HONORS, AND WEDDING BELLS

Beyoncé earned several other awards, honors, and nominations in 2007. *B'Day* was nominated for five Grammy Awards and won for the Best Contemporary R&B Album. She also won a trio of Soul Train Music Awards, including Best Female Singer and Best Song for "Déjà Vu," and became the first woman to win an International Artist Award at the 35th Annual American Music Awards.

In addition to the praise she received for her work in the film and music industries, Beyoncé was also drawing attention in other fields. *People* magazine named her one of the 10 best dressed celebrities of the year, and she also became the first female non-model, non-athlete to ever pose for the cover of the *Sports Illustrated* swimsuit issue. Now more than ever, Beyoncé was in the public eye, gaining fame and recognition for her musical talent, her acting, and her beauty.

Early in 2008, however, she stepped out of the spotlight and focused on her private life. On April 4, 2008, she quietly married longtime boyfriend Jay-Z in a private ceremony at his New York penthouse apartment. True to their natures, the bride and groom

KONSER

the Beyoncé experience

24 Ekim 2007
FENERBAHÇE ŞÜKRÜ
SARACOĞLU STADYUMU
Saat: 20.00

Photography by Leslie Kee

ECHOES production

As Beyoncé's international fame continued to grow, she launched a world tour to promote her album *B'Day*. In 2007 she was the first woman to win an International Artist Award at the American Music Awards. Her other music honors that year included five Grammy nominations and three Soul Train Music Awards.

only invited about 40 of their closest friends and family members, though the wedding ceremony was said to have included a nearly six-foot-tall cake and more than 70,000 white orchids. A florist who worked the event later told *Us Magazine* that the wedding looked like "heaven."

BECOMING SASHA FIERCE

For her next album, Beyoncé tapped into a different side of herself—a character known as Sasha Fierce. As she later explained, Sasha Fierce was an onstage role she played that allowed her to be more outgoing and aggressive while performing in front of large crowds. With *I Am . . . Sasha Fierce*, Beyoncé had hoped to harness some of that character's energy and channel it into a different type of effort, resulting in a two-CD set. One disc included more traditional Beyoncé music, while the other featured edgier, more experimental tracks.

I Am . . . Sasha Fierce was released on November 18, 2008. *Los Angeles Times* music critic Ann Powers had this to say about Beyoncé's third solo effort:

> **"Sasha's . . . about sonic complexity and challenging singing, rather than the cleaner, more open style of the Beyoncé tracks. . . . As a vocalist, Beyoncé seems more comfortable in Sasha's stilettos. Her performances on those cuts feel unforced and fun, like she's thinking on her feet. Stretching for deep meaning on the Beyoncé ballads, she risks sounding ponderous. . . . Still, when she finds the right balance, as on the first single 'If I Were a Boy,' she can be exquisite—accessing the timeless quality she's clearly bent on mastering."**

I Am . . . Sasha Fierce debuted at number one, making it three-for-three for Beyoncé albums opening atop the charts, and sold more than 480,000 copies in its first week. Several of the singles, including "Single Ladies (Put a Ring on It)" and "If I Were a Boy," went on to become major hits. It became one of the 10 best selling

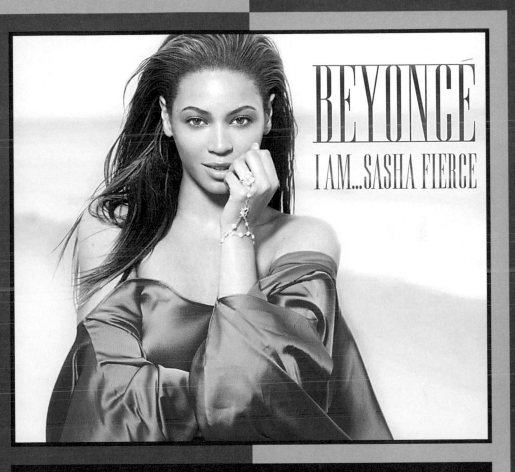

Beyoncé's two-CD album, *I am . . . Sasha Fierce*, debuted at the top of the charts. Critics and fans delighted in the mix of Beyoncé's signature style and new, edgier sounds. Several singles, such as "Single Ladies (Put a Ring on It)," were nationwide hits, and the album was one of 2008's top sellers.

albums of 2008, further cementing Beyoncé's legacy as one of the top female artists in music today.

CADILLAC RECORDS

Less than a month after the release of *I Am . . . Sasha Fierce*, Beyoncé's next movie hit theaters nationwide. The film was called *Cadillac Records*, and it came out on December 5, 2008. In the movie, Beyoncé plays music legend Etta James. She later donated her salary to Phoenix House rehabilitation centers in honor of Etta and her struggles with substance abuse. After all, as Beyoncé told Geoff Boucher of the *Los Angeles Times*, the role had special meaning for her:

In the film *Cadillac Records*, Beyoncé was challenged by the role of singer Etta James, who battled substance abuse for many years. Beyoncé was deservedly proud of her performance, and critics agreed, offering her Image Award and Satellite Award nominations.

"I wasn't sure I could even do it. I read Etta's book and watched every video of her I could find. I wanted to do her justice. She's a real woman that had guts and was unapologetic. . . . I wanted to make it real. . . . It was one of the hardest things I've ever done. . . . I'm the most proud of that movie, more than anything I've done so far."

Cadillac Records only earned about $8 million at the box office, but the film and Beyoncé's performance drew a lot of attention from critics and award committees. She received both Image Award and Satellite Award nominations for her portrayal of Etta James, and also received a Golden Globe nomination for her work on the song "Once in a Lifetime." She also sang Etta's classic "At Last" for the film's soundtrack. It would not be the last time she performed that particular song.

Etta James

Etta James was born in 1938 and went on to become one of the most famous female musicians of all time. She is a member of both the Rock and Roll Hall of Fame and the Blues Hall of Fame, and won four Grammys (including a Lifetime Achievement Award in 2002) and 17 Blues Music Awards during her colorful and expansive music career.

Her work influenced several well-known performers, including Janis Joplin, Diana Ross of The Supremes, Christina Aguilera, and Beyoncé. Among her most famous songs are "At Last," "The Wallflower" (which hit number one on the R&B charts), and "All I Could Do Was Cry." She famously battled drug abuse for much of her life, but managed to finally overcome addiction at the age of 50.

FORWARD INTO GREATNESS

Beyoncé's star continued to rise in 2009. In January, she was selected to perform "At Last" at one of the **inauguration** balls of U.S. President Barack Obama. In March, she launched a world tour in support of *I Am . . . Sasha Fierce* by performing a show in Edmonton, Alberta, Canada. April saw her appearance

Even world leaders find Beyoncé irresistible; she was honored to be invited to perform "At Last" during President Barack Obama's first Inaugural Ball. Beyoncé continues to amaze audiences with her music, acting, and business accomplishments, while she strives to be a role model for young women everywhere. Her future as a superstar is clearly limitless and bright.

in a commercial for the Nintendo DSi video game *Rhythm Heaven*, as well as the release of her most recent film, a romantic thriller called *Obsessed*. During that time, she also appeared on the cover of several magazines, including *Elle*, *Ebony*, and *Vogue*.

At one time a musical prodigy, Beyoncé had gone on to blossom into a superstar in every sense of the world. She had been recognized for her talents both in music and in theater, and had also become a role model to young girls everywhere—a responsibility that, as she once told Hannah Storm of CBS, she takes very seriously:

> **"[I want to be seen as] someone who works really hard, someone who is still human, and someone who is talented and wants to give good messages to other young people. Basically, my message is for kids and young girls to love themselves and not listen to all the negativity in the world."**

President Barack Obama

In January 2009, Barack Hussein Obama was sworn in as the 44th president of the United States of Amereica, and the first president of African-American heritage. President Obama was born on August 4, 1961, and earned a law degree from Harvard. He taught constitutional law at the University of Chicago and began his political career in 1996.

In 1997, Barack Obama served on the Illinois state legislature until 2004, when he ran for and won a seat in the United States Senate. In 2008, Congress.org ranked him as the 11th most powerful person in the Senate. Later that year, he was elected to the presidency, earning 365 out of 538 electoral votes and nearly 53% of the popular vote in the process. His inauguration took place on January 20, 2009.

What does the future hold for Beyoncé? Rumor has it that she is looking to reunite with Kelly Rowland and Michelle Williams for yet another Destiny's Child album. She has also publicly announced her desire to play Wonder Woman in an upcoming movie, though the odds of that actually happening are unknown. Obviously, future solo albums and world tours are in the cards as well. After all, Beyoncé is still a couple of years away from her 30th birthday. Despite having accomplished so much already, her career is still just getting started.

1981   Beyoncé Giselle Knowles is born on September 4 in Houston, Texas, to Mathew Knowles, an African American, and Tina Knowles, of Creole descent.

1988   Beyoncé enters and wins her first talent show. She performs John Lennon's "Imagine" and receives a standing ovation for her performance.

1989   Beyoncé becomes a part of the group Girl's Tyme, which also includes future Destiny's Child members Kelly Rowland, LeToya Luckett, and LaTavia Roberson.

1992   Girl's Tyme appears on the TV show *Star Search*. They perform a rap song and gain national television exposure but fail to win the competition.

1996   Beyoncé, Kelly, LeToya, and LaTavia, officially named Destiny's Child, sign with Columbia Records.

1997   Destiny's Child releases their first song, "Killing Time." It appears in the film *Men in Black*.

1998   Destiny's Child releases their first album, *Destiny's Child*, in February.

1999   The second Destiny's Child album, *The Writing's on the Wall*, is released on July 27. It produces two number one singles, "Bills, Bills, Bills" and "Say My Name."

2000   LeToya and LaTavia leave the group in February and are replaced by Michelle Williams and Farrah Franklin. Farrah leaves the group shortly thereafter.

       The new Destiny's Child lineup of Beyoncé, Kelly, and Michelle releases its first single in October. The song, "Independent Woman, Part I," spends 11 weeks atop the *Billboard* charts.

2001   The Destiny's Child album *Survivor* is released in May, and a Christmas-themed album entitled *8 Days of Christmas* comes out in October; the group announced that its members will temporarily part ways to work on solo projects.

       The group wins two Grammy Awards—Best R&B Vocal Performance by a Duo or Group and Best R&B Song for "Say My Name."

       Beyoncé becomes just the second woman ever to win the ASCAP Songwriter of the Year Award; She also lands a starring role in the made-for-TV musical *Carmen: A Hip Hopera*.

2002   Beyoncé stars as Foxxy Cleopatra in the film *Austin Powers in Goldmember*. The movie brings in more than $70 million during its opening weekend; meets and begins dating rapper and music producer Jay-Z.

2003 Beyoncé releases her first solo album, *Dangerously in Love*. It goes on to sell more than five million copies, and includes an appearance by Jay-Z on the song "Crazy in Love."

2004 Beyoncé sings the national anthem at Super Bowl XXXVIII; she wins five Grammy Awards, including Best R&B Song for "Crazy in Love."

She reunites with the other members of Destiny's Child for one final album, *Destiny Fulfilled*, and a farewell international tour.

2005 Beyoncé and her mother Tina open House of Deréon, a clothing business.

2006 Beyoncé stars in two films, *The Pink Panther* and *Dreamgirls*.

She releases her second solo album, *B'Day*; it hits number one in its first week and includes the song "Irreplaceable," which spends 10 consecutive weeks atop the charts.

2007 Beyoncé wins the Grammy for Best Contemporary R&B Album for *B'Day* and is the first woman to win the International Artist Award at the American Music Awards.

She is named one of the 10 best dressed celebrities of the year by *People* magazine and graces the cover of the *Sports Illustrated* swimsuit issue.

2008 Beyoncé marries Jay-Z on April 4.

She releases her third solo album, *I Am . . . Sasha Fierce*, which debuts at number one on the *Billboard* charts.

In December, the film *Cadillac Records* is released, with Beyoncé in the role of musical legend Etta James.

2009 Beyoncé performs at the inauguration of President Barack Obama in January.

On February 12, 2009, she wins the NAACP Image Award for Outstanding Female Artist. She also performs her hit song "Halo" during the show.

In March, she kicks off a world tour in support of *I Am . . . Sasha Fierce* by performing a live show in Edmonton, Alberta, Canada.

In April, her latest film *Obsessed* hits theaters nationwide, and she appears in a national television commercial for the new Nintendo video game *Rhythm Heaven*.

Albums

1998 *Destiny's Child* (with Destiny's Child)

1999 *The Writing's on the Wall* (with Destiny's Child)

2001 *Survivor* (with Destiny's Child)
8 Days of Christmas (with Destiny's Child)

2003 *Dangerously in Love*

2004 *Destiny Fulfilled* (with Destiny's Child)

2006 *B'Day*

2008 *I Am . . . Sasha Fierce*

Number-One Singles

2003 "Crazy in Love"
"Baby Boy"

2005 "Check on It"

2006 "Irreplaceable"

2008 "Single Ladies (Put a Ring on It)"

Movies

2001 *Carmen: A Hip-Hopera*

2002 *Austin Powers in Goldmember*

2003 *The Fighting Temptations*

2006 *The Pink Panther*
Dreamgirls

2008 *Cadillac Records*

2009 *Obsessed*

Awards

2001   ASCAP Pop Music Award, Songwriter of the Year
Grammy Awards for Best R&B Performance by a Duo or Group with Vocals
and Best R&B Song

2002   Grammy Award, Best R&B Performance by a Duo or Group with Vocals
BRIT Award, Best International Group
NAACP Image Award, Outstanding Group

2003   Billboard Music Awards for Best New Female Artist and Best New R&B Artist

2004   Grammy Awards for Best Female R&B Vocal Performance, Best R&B Performance
by a Duo or Group with Vocals, Best R&B Song, Best Contemporary R&B
Album, and Best Rap/Sung Collaboration

2006   Soul Train Music Award, Quincy Jones Award for Outstanding Career
Achievements

2007   Grammy Award, Best Contemporary R&B Album
BET Award, Best Female R&B Artist and Video of the Year
Kids' Choice Awards for Favorite Female Singer and Favorite Song

2008   Demand International Entertainer of the Year
World Music Award, Outstanding Contribution to the Arts

2009   NAACP Image Award, Outstanding Female Artist
Kids' Choice Award, Favorite Song

adversity—going through difficult times or facing challenges.

ascended—climbed; rose up to.

collaborated—worked together or teamed up with.

dejected—mildly depressed; disappointed.

diva—a successful and usually glamorous female performer.

domestically—within one's home country or nation.

epitomizing—serving as the perfect example of something.

hiatus—a break or time away from something.

inauguration—a ceremony in which a political official is sworn into office.

moniker—another word for a name.

nominated—selected as a finalist for an award or honor.

philanthropist—a person who tries to make the world a better place by giving out funds to charities.

portfolio—a record of a person's accomplishments, usually in an artistic field.

segregation—the separation of people due to physical characteristics, such as the color of their skin.

speculate—to guess or make predictions based on little evidence; to wonder.

Books

Arenofsky, Janice. *Beyoncé Knowles: A Biography*. Santa Barbara, California: Greenwood, 2009.

Knowles, Beyoncé, Kelly Rowland, and Michelle Williams. *Soul Survivors: The Official Autobiography of Destiny's Child*. New York: HarperEntertainment, 2002.

Knowles, Tina and Zoe Alexander. *Destiny's Style: Bootylicious Fashion, Beauty, and Lifestyle Secrets from Destiny's Child*. New York: HarperEntertainment, 2002.

Tracy, Kathleen. *Beyoncé*. Hockessin, Delaware: Mitchell Lane, 2004.

Waters, Rosa. *Beyoncé*. Broomall, Pennsylvania: Mason Crest, 2007.

Webster, Christine. *Beyoncé Knowles*. New York: Weigl Publishers, 2005.

Web Sites

http://www.Beyoncéonline.com/

This is Beyoncé's official homepage. Here you can check out all of the latest news about her career, view a calendar of upcoming events, check out photos and videos (including some submitted by fans), visit the forums and connect with other Beyoncé fans, download desktop wallpaper and buddy icons for your PC, and more.

http://www.houseofdereon.com/

The Web site for Beyoncé and Tina Knowles's business venture, House of Deréon, is another must-see Internet location. Here, you can get background on the business, including the rich Creole heritage that helped inspire it, and scope out the latest fashion offerings in their online "Lookbook."

http://www.destinyschild.com/index3.html

While the group may or may not be reuniting for another album, their official Web site is still alive and well. In addition to reading the group's biographical information, you can check out their music, videos, photos, and more. You can also download a cell phone dancing game featuring several Destiny's Child hits.

http://www.weloveBeyoncé.com

Finally, if you want to find the ultimate place to hang out with other fans of Beyoncé, her music and her movies, make sure you stop by the official homepage of her fan club. Please note, however, that you need to register in order to access the full Web site.

page

2:	Kevin Winter/Getty Images	**36:**	Kevin Mazur/WireImage
6:	LOC/PRMM	**39:**	Terry Schmitt/UPI Photo
9:	Jeff Kravitz/FilmMagic	**41:**	(top left) Chris Graythen/Getty Images
10:	Kevin Winter/Getty Images for NAACP	**41:**	(top right) Kathy Hutchins/Hutchins Photo
12:	Vogue/NMI		
15:	StarMax Photos	**41:**	(bottom left) Kathy Hutchins/Hutchins Photo
17:	StarMax Photos		
18:	StarMax Photos	**41:**	(bottom right) London Entertainment/ Splash News
21:	Columbia Records/NMI		
22:	London Entertainment/SMP	**42:**	Scott Gries/Getty Images
25:	Mirrorpix Photos	**45:**	Zuma Press
27:	Columbia Records/NMI	**46:**	DreamWorks/Paramount/NMI
28:	Columbia Records/NMI	**49:**	New Millennium Images
31:	Columbia Records/NMI	**51:**	Columbia Records/NMI
32:	Deutsche Presse Agentur	**52:**	TriStar Pictures/NMI
35:	New Line Cinema/NMI	**54:**	Suzanne Day/USAF/PRMM

Front cover: SIPA Press

ABOUT THE AUTHOR

Chuck Bednar is an author and freelance writer from Ohio. He has been writing professionally since 1997 and has written more than 1,500 published nonfiction articles. Bednar is also the author of eight books, including the *Tony Parker* and *Tim Duncan* entries in Mason Crest's MODERN ROLE MODELS series, as well as SUPERSTARS OF PRO FOOTBALL: *Tony Romo*. He is currently employed by Bright Hub (www.brighthub.com) as the Managing Editor for their Nintendo Wii Web site.